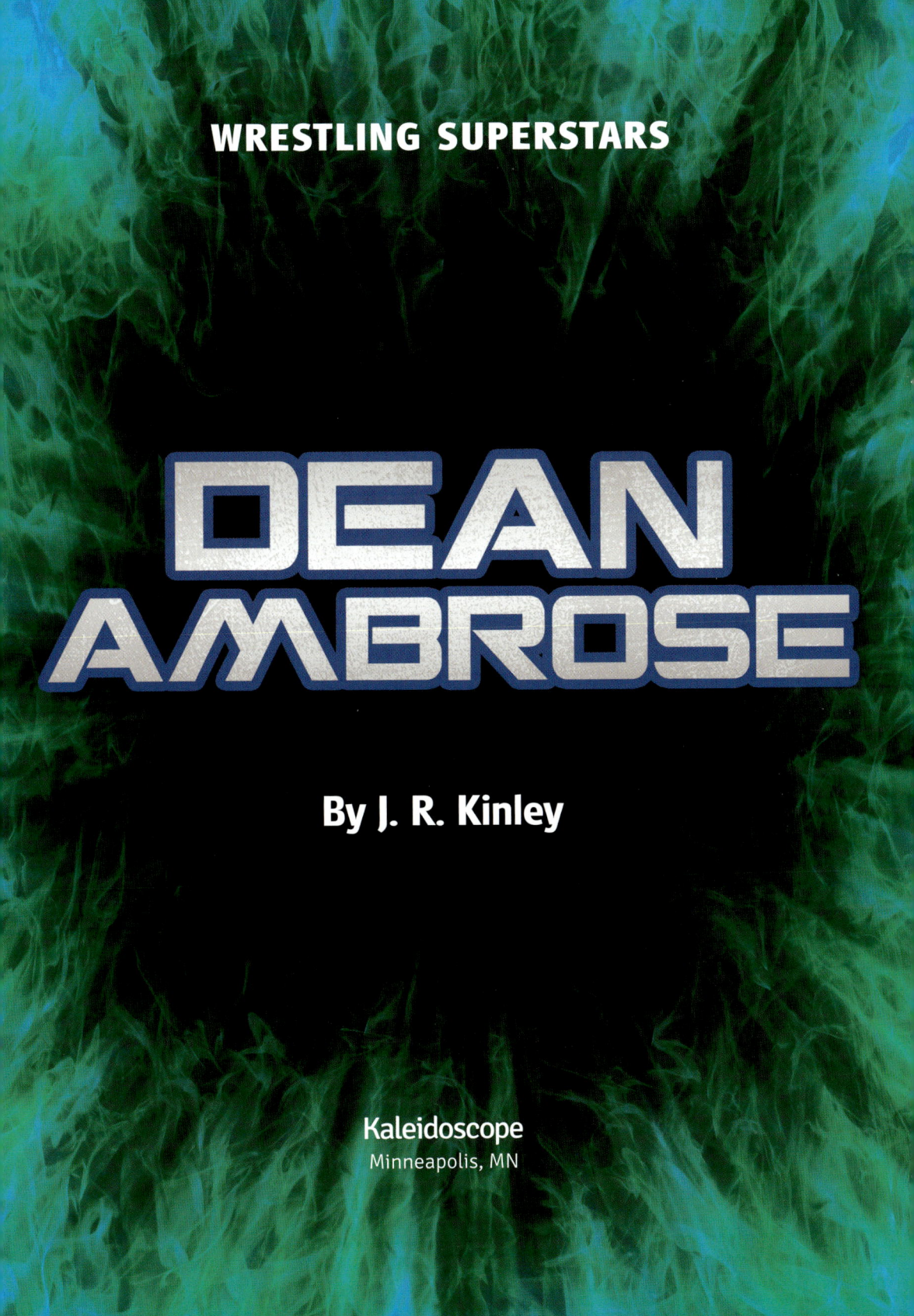

WRESTLING SUPERSTARS

DEAN AMBROSE

By J. R. Kinley

Kaleidoscope
Minneapolis, MN

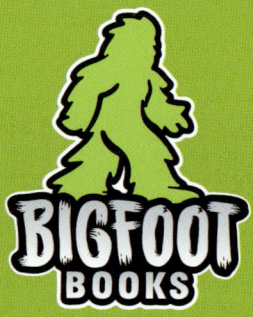

The Quest for Discovery Never Ends

....

This edition first published in 2020 by Kaleidoscope Publishing, Inc.

No part of this publication may be reproduced in whole or in part without written permission of the publisher.

For information regarding permission, write to
Kaleidoscope Publishing, Inc.
6012 Blue Circle Drive
Minnetonka, MN 55343

Library of Congress Control Number
2019940196

ISBN
978-1-64519-098-1 (library bound)
978-1-64494-224-6 (paperback)
978-1-64519-188-9 (ebook)

Text copyright © 2020 by Kaleidoscope Publishing, Inc. All-Star Sports, Bigfoot Books, and associated logos are trademarks and/or registered trademarks of Kaleidoscope Publishing, Inc.

Printed in the United States of America.

Bigfoot lurks within one of the images in this book. It's up to you to find him!

TABLE OF CONTENTS

Chapter 1: The Shield's Debut **4**

Chapter 2: "Being Me All the Time" **10**

Chapter 3: A Brawler **16**

Chapter 4: Grand Slam **22**

Beyond the Book 28
Research Ninja 29
Further Resources 30
Glossary 31
Index 32
Photo Credits 32
About the Author 32

CHAPTER 1

The Shield's Debut

It was November 2012. Dean Ambrose was new to World Wrestling Entertainment (WWE). He had trained hard in NXT. NXT is a **promotion**. It prepares wrestlers for WWE.

Ambrose wasn't alone. He was with wrestlers Seth Rollins and Roman Reigns. They were friends from NXT.

They were **debuting** together. They would work as a team. They called themselves the Shield. People said fans would hate them. But they decided to work hard. They wanted to be the best thing on the show.

Ambrose, left, Reigns, center, and Rollins, right, worked together to make an impression at their WWE debut.

CM Punk, John Cena, and Ryback were wrestling. The match was in full swing. Fans cheered for Ryback. It looked like he would win. He used his Shell Shocked move. It knocked both Cena and Punk to the ground.

Suddenly, three men ran through the crowd. It was Ambrose and his two friends. They dressed in all black. They leapt into the ring. Ambrose was a **brawler**. He attacked Ryback with punches. Then all three worked together. They slammed Ryback through an announcer's table. Punk took his chance. He pinned Cena. He won! The Shield's **alliance** helped him. Ambrose's debut was a success.

FUN FACT
The Shield wrestlers wore black turtlenecks for their debut, but switched to combat outfits for later matches.

The Shield was considered to be a dominant group in the WWE.

Ambrose became the main speaker for the group. He said they were the Shield. They fought against unfairness.

While the Shield was active, the wrestlers took down big names in WWE like Daniel Bryan.

They helped some wrestlers win. And they took down big names in pro wrestling. "We **dominated** WWE," Ambrose said. The Shield broke up in 2014. But Ambrose felt they went out on top.

CHAPTER 2

"Being Me All the Time"

Dean Ambrose's real name is Jonathan Good. He grew up in a small Ohio apartment and lived with his mom and sister. Ambrose was always a fan of pro wrestling. He would watch hours of wrestling videos. Bret Hart was his favorite. He liked that Hart outsmarted other wrestlers.

Growing up, Ambrose admired Canadian American wrestler Bret "the Hitman" Hart.

Some wrestlers get their start working with independent promotions.

One day, he passed a phone pole. He noticed a flyer. It was for a local wrestling show. He decided to go. He liked that he could sit up so close. He was right by the ring. At the show he saw an ad for a pro wrestling camp. It was called Heartland Wrestling Association (HWA). Ambrose felt like a light shone down on him. He knew he would go there. But he wasn't old enough yet. He worked there instead. He swept floors and sold popcorn.

Soon, he turned eighteen. He started training with HWA. He debuted in 2004 as Jon Moxley. He wrestled with HWA for many years. He also spent time in other promotions. It wasn't always easy. He imagined wrestling in WWE. He pictured big cheering crowds and huge arenas. But instead he wrestled in high school gyms. Small crowds watched. He tried out for WWE a few times. WWE turned him down. He could have given up. But he kept wrestling. Failures made him work harder.

His confidence grew. He said, "I just started being me all the time." He won matches as Jon Moxley. He held many titles with Combat Zone Wrestling (CZW).

One day, Ambrose got a call. It was from WWE. He thought it was a friend's prank at first. But it was real. WWE offered him a spot in Florida Championship Wrestling (FCW). FCW would later become NXT. Ambrose wouldn't let this chance slip by.

He started wrestling as Dean Ambrose. He made the WWE main roster in 2012.

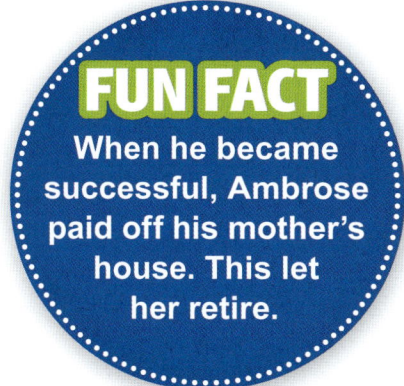

FUN FACT
When he became successful, Ambrose paid off his mother's house. This let her retire.

Ambrose's signature moves have earned him many titles over the course of his wrestling career.

CHAPTER 3

A Brawler

It was 2013. Kofi Kingston had the US title. Ambrose wanted it for himself. In their match, they showed off their signature moves. These are the moves that a wrestler is known for. Both wrestlers had trained hard. They learned how to do these moves as safely as possible. But the moves were still risky.

The bell rang. The match began with holds and throws. Kingston pushed Ambrose into the ropes. Ambrose bounced right back. He knocked Kingston to the ground. Ambrose often rebounds off the ropes. He's even known for a move called the rebound lariat. For that move, he bounces off the ropes. Then he hits his opponent with a **clothesline**. The ropes help him gain **momentum**. This helps him deliver stronger attacks.

Ambrose was still new to WWE when he faced US Champion Kofi Kingston in 2013.

Ambrose often jumps from the top ropes into an elbow drop.

Kingston punched Ambrose over and over. The crowd counted the punches out. Then Kingston charged. Ambrose kicked him away. But he charged again. Ambrose hit a clothesline. Kingston fell to the mat. Ambrose did an elbow drop. He uses elbow drops in many of his matches. He fell onto Kingston with his arm. He slammed his elbow into Kingston's face. Ambrose taunted him. He said, "I'm the US champ, Kofi."

But Kingston started to get the upper hand. He hit Ambrose with a dropkick. Later, he kicked Ambrose in the jaw. Ambrose fell out of the ring. But Ambrose wouldn't go down so easily. He used his signature Dirty Deeds. He put Kingston in a headlock. Then he fell forward. He slammed Kingston's face into the mat. Dirty Deeds finished Kingston off. Ambrose won by **pinfall**. He won the US title!

The next year, Ambrose changed Dirty Deeds. He didn't slam the opponent forward anymore. Instead, he pulled the opponent backward. He still smashed their face into the mat, though.

FUN FACT
Dean Ambrose has the nickname "Lunatic Fringe." He likes to appear mad and crazed.

In 2015, Ambrose faced Kevin Owens. Owens was Intercontinental Champion. The wrestlers brawled. Ambrose took a hard slam. But he kept fighting. Owens threw him into the ropes. But Ambrose bounced back. He leapfrogged over Owens. It was his chance to show off the new Dirty Deeds. Ambrose hooked his arms under Owens's arms. He fell backward, pulling Owens with him. He slammed Owens down.

Owens struggled. He finally got up. He tried to pin Ambrose. But Ambrose kicked out. He flipped Owens to the mat. He pinned him for the three-count. Dirty Deeds helped Ambrose win his first Intercontinental Title.

Kevin Owens

Ambrose showed off his title belt.

CHAPTER 4

Grand Slam

The WWE Grand Slam Title is rare. It's only given to wrestlers who win four different WWE titles. Most never win it. But Ambrose had a chance. He'd won three WWE titles. He needed to be tag team champion. That would earn him the Grand Slam.

It was August 2017. Ambrose and Seth Rollins teamed up. They faced Cesaro and Sheamus for the Raw Tag Team Championship.

Rollins and Ambrose, left, took on Sheamus and Cesaro, right, at the August 2017 SummerSlam event.

CAREER HIGHLIGHTS

2004

2004–2011
Ambrose trains and competes with Heartland Wrestling Association. He also wrestles for International Pro Wrestling and Combat Zone Wrestling.

2011
Ambrose begins wrestling with the FCW developmental roster, which will become NXT.

2011

2012

2012
Ambrose debuts on the WWE main roster with the Shield.

2013
Ambrose defeats Kofi Kingston for the WWE United States Championship. He holds the title for 351 days.

2013

2015

2015
Ambrose wins his first WWE Intercontinental Championship. He will go on to win it two more times.

2016
Ambrose defeats Rollins for the WWE Championship.

2016

2018
Ambrose and Rollins win a second Tag Team Championship.

2018

2019

2019
Ambrose announces that he'll take a break from wrestling with WWE.

The bell rang. Ambrose and Cesaro started in the ring. Ambrose put Cesaro in a hold. Cesaro reached over to tag in Sheamus. Sheamus took his place. Ambrose locked his arms around Sheamus. He slammed him down.

Sheamus, left, and Cesaro, right, have been opponents in the past.

The match went on. Cesaro knocked Ambrose out of the ring. Sheamus dropped him with his Brogue Kick. Ambrose seemed to be out. Rollins was on his own. Sheamus and Cesaro smashed him onto the arena floor. They beat him up.

Ambrose rose up. He climbed the ropes. He held out his hand. Rollins crawled toward him. Sheamus and Cesaro tried to stop him. But he fought through. He finally tagged his partner in. Ambrose and Rollins took over. But Sheamus lifted Ambrose on his back. He went for his finishing move.

FUN FACT
Dean Ambrose is married to Renee Young, a WWE commentator.

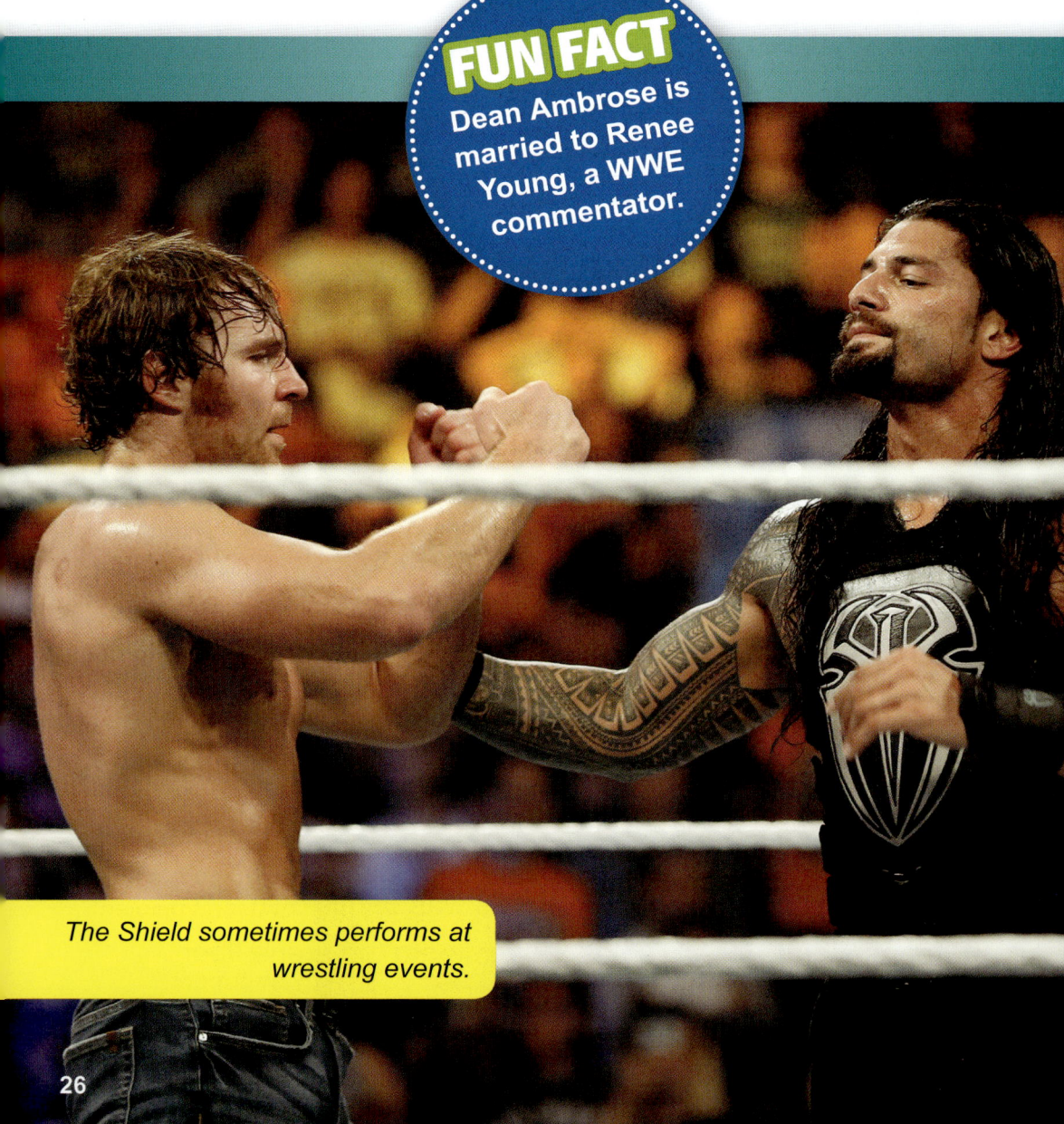

The Shield sometimes performs at wrestling events.

Rollins saw what was happening. He had to stop Sheamus. He jumped up. He hooked his legs around Cesaro. Then he sent him flying into Sheamus. Ambrose finished the match. He grabbed Sheamus. He fell backward. He slammed Sheamus to the mat face-first. Dirty Deeds! Ambrose and Rollins won!

The winners did their old Shield fist bump. They were tag team champions. Ambrose won the Grand Slam title. He couldn't have done it without his friend.

Ambrose made an announcement in 2019. He was taking a break from wrestling with WWE. WWE hopes he'll return one day. But no matter what, he'll be a wrestling superstar.

THE RETURN OF MOXLEY

Dean Ambrose left WWE in 2019. He changed his name on his social media accounts. It appeared as Jon Moxley. He released a video. It showed him training and spelled out "M-O-X." It was a hint. He would still wrestle. But not as Dean Ambrose. His old Jon Moxley character would return.

BEYOND THE BOOK

After reading the book, it's time to think about what you learned. Try the following exercises to jumpstart your ideas.

THINK

THAT'S NEWS TO ME. Dean Ambrose teamed up with Seth Rollins and Roman Reigns for the Shield. Consider how news sources could fill in more information on the Shield's first wrestling match. What new information could be found in news articles? Where could you go to find those news sources?

CREATE

SHARPEN YOUR RESEARCH SKILLS. Dean Ambrose liked learning about the history of pro wrestling and old pro wrestling stars. Where could you go in the library, or who could you talk to, to learn more about the history of pro wrestling? Create a research plan that outlines your next steps for research.

SHARE

WHAT'S YOUR OPINION?. Dean Ambrose says that the Shield "dominated WWE" for some time. Do you agree with this? Provide evidence from the text that supports your position. Share your opinion and evidence with a friend. Does your friend find your argument convincing?

GROW

DRAWING CONNECTIONS. Think about alliances. Draw a diagram that shows how alliances relate to professional wrestling. How does understanding alliances help you to better understand professional wrestling?

RESEARCH NINJA

Visit *www.ninjaresearcher.com/0981* to learn how to take your research skills and book report writing to the next level!

RESEARCH

DIGITAL LITERACY TOOLS

SEARCH LIKE A PRO
Learn about how to use search engines to find useful websites.

FACT OR FAKE?
Discover how you can tell a trusted website from an untrustworthy resource.

TEXT DETECTIVE
Explore how to zero in on the information you need most.

SHOW YOUR WORK
Research responsibly—learn how to cite sources.

WRITE

GET TO THE POINT
Learn how to express your main ideas.

PLAN OF ATTACK
Learn prewriting exercises and create an outline.

DOWNLOADABLE REPORT FORMS

Further Resources

BOOKS

Black, Jake. *WWE Ultimate Superstar Guide*. WWE / Penguin Random House / DK, 2018.

Borth, Teddy. *Dean Ambrose: The Lunatic Fringe*. Abdo, 2018.

Price, Sean. *The Kids' Guide to Pro Wrestling*. Edge Books, 2012.

WEBSITES

Factsurfer.com gives you a safe, fun way to find more information.

1. Go to www.factsurfer.com.
2. Enter "Dean Ambrose" into the search box and click 🔍.
3. Select your book cover to see a list of related websites.

Glossary

alliance: People or groups form an alliance when they join together for a common goal. Ambrose, Rollins, and Reigns formed an alliance against other wrestlers.

brawler: A brawler is a rough fighter who uses kicks and punches and often takes matches outside of the ring. Some fans say Ambrose is a brawler because of his hard-hitting fighting style.

clothesline: To perform a clothesline, a wrestler hits an opponent in the neck or chest with an extended arm. For his rebound lariat, Ambrose bounces off the ropes and attacks his opponent with a clothesline.

debuting: People or groups of people who are debuting are making their first formal public appearance or entrance. Ambrose and the Shield were debuting together.

dominated: A person or group has dominated an event or organization if they were very important or powerful within it. The Shield dominated WWE after its debut.

momentum: Momentum is strength or power built by something moving. Ambrose rebounds off of the ropes for his moves so that he can gain momentum for his attacks.

pinfall: A pinfall is the official count to three in a pin, resulting in a decision. Dean Ambrose won the match by pinfall.

promotion: A wrestling promotion is a company that organizes wrestling events. WWE is a popular pro wrestling promotion.

Index

Cena, John, 6
Cesaro, 22, 24–27
clothesline, 16–17, 19

debut, 5–6, 13, 23

Grand Slam, 22, 27

Hart, Bret, 10

Intercontinental Title, 20, 23

Kingston, Kofi, 16, 19, 23

Owens, Kevin, 20

pinfall, 19

Reigns, Roman, 4
Rollins, Seth, 4, 22–23, 25–27

Shield, the, 5–6, 8–9, 23, 27
signature moves, 16, 19

tag team, 22–23, 27

PHOTO CREDITS

The images in this book are reproduced through the courtesy of: Marc Pfitzenreuter/Getty Images Sport/Getty Images, front cover; SnakeMannn/Splash News/Newscom, pp. 3, 14–15; Matt Roberts/Zuma Press/Icon Sportswire, pp. 4–5; JLJ/ZOJ/JLN Photography/WENN/Newscom, pp. 6–7, 8–9, 17; Kleber Cordeiro/Shutterstock Images, p. 10; Jean-Marc Mouchet/DPPI/Icon Sportswire, pp. 10–11; juliet_eden/iStockphoto, pp. 12–13; CD1/Carrie Devorah/WENN/Newscom, p. 16; Sylvain Lefevre/Getty Images Sport/Getty Images, p. 18; Christian Bertrand/Shutterstock Images, p. 20; Philippe Huguen/AFP/Getty Images, pp. 20–21, 23 (belt), 30; Adam Hunger/Invision for 2K Games/AP Images, p. 22; Red Line Editorial, p. 23 (timeline); A Fraioli/Splash News/Newscom, pp. 24–25; JP Yim/Getty Images Entertainment/Getty Images, p. 26.

ABOUT THE AUTHOR

J. R. Kinley is a writer and artist. She is part of a wrestling family from Ohio in one of the top wrestling regions in the nation. Her husband, Shaun Kinley, former NCAA wrestler at The Ohio State University, coaches at the nationally ranked St. Edward High School. Together, they operate Kinley Studio.